InspireMe

Kirsty Heaton

BookLeaf Publishing

Presentation by *BookLeaf Publishing*

Web: www.bookleafpub.com

E-mail: info@bookleafpub.com

ISBN: 9789357440981

First edition 2023

My three beautiful boys,

*For always showing me the lighter side to
life and truely living in the moment*

This will pass

Alone with her thoughts
How can I do this?
Carry this weight?
Her back hunched over,
Her eyes sunken
It was the dead of night
But there was no rest
The moon listened
The stars heard
And in that moment
They lent a spark
To light her heart
To give her a kick start
"This moment will pass
With strength and courage"
They whispered
'Go soar my little shooting star"

A note for you

The ones who have cried in the shower
So no one knows
The ones who knew they couldnt stay, but
thought they couldn't go
That share a bed
But still felt cold
Practiced your smiles
For a show
The reflection of you
Who isn't
But who you made just to get through
It's okay now
The coast is clear
Let go of her hand
It's safe now to be you
We have cried together
Our silent tears
We make an army
You have no idea!
Go be you
Enough fear
Go be fierce
Go be abundant
Go make that life that was always yours
We are rooting for you

Be that nova
Go be you!

Beautiful Soul

Hey there beautiful soul
I just wanted to tell you, so you know

Things are okay,
Try to let go

Don't be so hard on yourself
Beautiful soul

Your strength will move mountains
Your voice will part clouds
Your vision will inspire others to grow
And your heart?
Place your hand on your chest
Close your eyes, just for a moment

Feel that beat
Hear that sound
Thats your passion that flows within

Believe in yourself, you beautiful soul

You got this
I promise

The sea

Like the sea
Our hearts run deep
Wild and choppy
Calm and tranquil

Like the sea our hearts are destructive and fierce
Freeing and forgiving

Just like the sea
Our hearts can be intimidating and violent
Sacred and life giving

Just like the sea
Let your heart flow
Let your love flow
Let it never stay in one state too long
Let it wash over you
Take a note
Your heart is just like the sea
It can be all forces but never too long

Tiny star

Tiny star in the midnight
light
So unaware of the awe
you gather
The comfort you create
The hope you keep
The dreams you cradle
The calm you bring

Tiny star in the midnight
light
So unaware of the
beauty you hold
The power you muster
The fires you spark

Oh darling little star in
the midnight light
So unaware
Maybe that is why you
Shine so bright

Just one thing

If I could give you just one thing
It would be knowledge

The knowledge to know how brave you are
The knowledge to know the strength you hold
The knowledge to know how loved you are

If I could give you just one thing
It would be comfort

The comfort in your abilities
The comfort from deep within
The comfort of knowing your soul

If I could give you just one thing
It would be love
Love that cradles you through your darkest times
Love that comes with passion
Love that you can share without fear

If I could give you just one thing
It would be confidence

Confidence that even when you are so wrong
You know you can make it right

Confidence in your path
Confidence in yourself
Confidence in how you carry your head high

If I could just give you one thing

I know

9

I know you have the confidence to see this
through
I know you have the strength to be you
I know you have the talent to make it work
You have the will deep in your heart
Stand up straight
Hold your head high
Take a moment
Realign
You have everything you need
Right here
Right now
I promise it's there
All in you

A dark November

She had a flicker in her eyes
A fire ember
But she was stuck in a dark November

Her voice was strong but with a quiver
She had fooled herself and everyone with her

She could feel this flicker
We could see the ember

She knew her path
The strength she had within her

But ....

How do you light a flicker
On a dark November ?

Learning

I am learning to let go of things that don't serve
me
Heart ache
Pain
Things that aren't aligned

I am learning to let go and heal the things that
are no good
People
Places
Things that aren't seen by the naked eye

I am beautiful
I am divine
I'm gonna make what is meant to be mine

I'm gonna find peace
I'm gonna find love
It's just gonna take some time

Dip your toe in

Open your heart
Open your mind
Come take a stroll with me
I know you're hurting
I know that you're yearning
For something
Something thing deeper than you and me
Come take that first step
Dip your toe in
I promise
The water is fine
Close your eyes
Trust your heart
There's something in your eyes
Something beautiful
Something brighter
Go take a look
I see it shining
It's just waiting for you to dip your toe in

Safe and sound

Lay your burdens down
You're safe and sound with me
Right here, right now
No worries or fears
Let's Be free, I wanna be clear
You're safe and sound with me
Got to feel that love
Let's be at peace, just you and me
Let's be free
Let your body and mind pause time
I want you to know
I want you to feel how safe and sound you are
with me
In this moment
In this space
In the lines between the words we share
You're safe and sound with me

Smile

Smile
Take some time
Find that place
Clear you mind
You're doing fine
I know your head is heavy
Doubt
Worries
Fears
You don't feel perfect
And that's fine
Relax your shoulders
Put down your shield
It's not always a battle that's up hill
Just take some time
Go and clear your mind
No worries
No fears
No doubts
Will ever be a match for you
So smile my dear
It's gonna be fine

13

13 and so lost
She didn't have a clue
Not a friend to call or a 50/50 option
She was 13 and lost
Wolves in sheeps clothing
Waiting for their time
Holding out their hands
With promiscs of;
A moment of care
A moment of safety
A moment of love
But she didn't have a clue
So she grabbed these hands
But only found claws
They dug deep ,the marks never gone
13 and clueless ,lost and forgotten
"How could she be so foolish" people will mutter
"She should know better" they will whisper
But she was only 13 and clueless
And the pack was tightened in
But scars heal
Time passes
She found her own love
Her own safety

And her own care
For she is no longer 13 and foolish
She's a warrior
A fighter

Taking part

When you just can't win
Always second place
Giving it your all
But always just short
Do or don't
It doesn't matter
These are the times
That really count
Sometimes you can't measure
Winner and losers
It doesn't always mean a medal
Or a cheering crowd
Every now and again
You have to be your own cheerleader
Make your own medal
It really doesn't matter
Life isn't a game
And even if it was
It's the taking part that counts

Can we restart?

What a day
A bumpy start
Running late
Sweaty palms
Every red light
Traffic too!
What a day
What a start
Can we start over?
Hi my name is …
Of course you can
How do you do ?

Cloud 9

I am sipping on sunshine
Checked into cloud 9
Smiling like that Cheshire cat
While I jump over the moon
I met Larry
He was very happy
I'm here on top of the world
Having a whale of a time!

He was the sun

He was the sun
I was the moon
Never in the same light
But not one without the other
A constant cycle
Of light and dark
Hot and cold
He was the sun
And I the moon
Then I knew
A planet and a star
Can't cross paths

Playing with fire

Playing with fire
"It's hot, don't touch!"
My mother would mutter
"Don't be playing with fire!"
Still I go in
For a poke
Why with a warning, would you still play with
fire?
There's a wonder
A magic
That draws us in
We have to find out
What happens if you play with fire?

The river

Sit down by the river
Take your time
It's a charming little spot
To free your mind
Embrace the harmony
Take your time
Come sit down by the river

Something bigger

Your heart is heavy
So was mine
Here we are
Come together
All looking for something better
You and me
On different paths
But wanting something bigger

Maybe

Maybe we sparkle from afar
Like a butterfly unable to see it's wings
A star unaware of it's glisten from afar

Maybe we twinkle from afar
Everything has beauty
Just not seen by all

www.ingramcontent.com/pod-product-compliance
Lightning Source LLC
Chambersburg PA
CBHW070733160726
48003CB00006BA/2478